Dear Beverly,
   God bless you!
I hope you enjoy
the book.
   love
   Art

Women in Ministry:
I Commend To You My

Sister

By Arthur Jaggard

Forward by Kate Harvey

1663 LIBERTY DRIVE, SUITE 200
BLOOMINGTON, INDIANA 47403
(800) 839-8640
WWW.AUTHORHOUSE.COM

First published by AuthorHouse 03/30/05

ISBN: 1-4208-3472-X (sc)

Printed in the United States of America
Bloomington, Indiana

This book is printed on acid-free paper.

Table of Contents

Dedicated to Sarah Elizabeth Jaggard

In memory of
Doradean Rinard

With special thanks to my parents Arthur and Lois Jaggard, Rev. Victor Powell, Rev. Kate Harvey, and The American Baptist Minister's Council

Foreword

How does the Word of God instruct us on the still somewhat contentious issue of women in ministry? After all, that is the first question to raise when any traditional view is challenged within the Church. It is all well and good for the heart to be tugged toward a new thing and even for experience to validate its warrant, but if the Bible does not support transformation of what we have considered traditionally held convictions, then we must keep to our old ways.

I vividly recall a conversation in the mid 1970's when as a woman my heart was tugged toward ordained ministry and I entered seminary seeking to discern where God was calling me. A pastor of a nearby church from another denomination said flatly, "You know that you were born to become a pastor. Forget trying to make sense of that in terms of the Bible. Just do it."

But that is precisely what a follower of Jesus Christ cannot do. One cannot ever discount the Bible. However, what one can and must do is go back to the relevant biblical texts with the filters removed that dictate what those texts must surely mean. In other words, we must look with new eyes at the texts we have been taught to see as prohibitive. Miraculously, the Living Word of God always instructs us in ever new times and circumstances, if we allow it freedom from the shackles of ancient interpretations that when tested prove invalid.

As Jesus himself said, "I still have many things to say to you, but you cannot bear them now. When the Spirit of truth comes, he will guide you into all the truth..." (John 15:12-13a)

In *Women in Ministry: I Commend to You My Sister*, Art Jaggard brings together the true biblical witness concerning women in ministry with true stories of women in ministry. Together they serve to open the mind and the heart to the reality that God calls women as well as men to ordained ministry and pours out upon both gifts for ministry.

During my 25 plus years of ministry I have observed that the most effective way to open the doors of the Church to receive the fullness of God's blessing through ordained leadership is for men to advocate on behalf of women in ministry and for women simply to minister faithfully and effectively. Then ears can open because the advocate is not a woman who might seem to be beating her own drum and the minister in question is an excellent servant of God who just happens to be a woman. Then support of women in ministry is seen less as a justice issue of advocacy for women as victims of prejudice, and more a source of some of the best leadership God is yearning to offer to the Church.

That's what it comes down to: where will the Church find the best leadership for today and tomorrow? The Ministers Council of the American Baptist Churches commends to you this book as you seek to answer that question for your own local congregation. The Ministers Council, the professional association of ministerial leaders within the denomination, defines its constituency and mission as: "We are women and men who advocate for and covenant with each other to deepen our spiritual journey and to increase our effectiveness, as persons who are accepting the call of God and church for the advancement of the mission of the church of Jesus Christ and to proclaim His truth in a prophetic voice as led by the Holy Spirit." In our journey together we have discovered that God's Church in the twenty-first century is in need of excellence in leadership, and some of the best do just happen to be women.

May this book serve for you and your congregation as an instrument of the Spirit who leads us ever deeper into truth.

Kate Harvey
Executive Director
Ministers Council
American Baptist Churches

Introduction:

Before beginning a book like this it is important to keep things in context. There are several specific pieces of information that will help do that.

First, your author is an Area Minister for American Baptist Churches. He serves as a pastor to pastors and a resource for the churches in his Area. An Area Minister would be called a Director of Missions in the Southern Baptist tradition and in the United Methodist Church he or she would called a District Superintendent.

This situation occupies a sort of denominational middle ground. Though American Baptists in general are every bit as Biblically oriented as any other group, they are so much smaller than some that larger dominant groups can describe them as something other than Biblical when it suits them.

On the other hand the denomination is by no means small. It includes a million and a half people throughout the United States. This gives the denomination an inclination to try to find its own way through difficult theological issues with out defining themselves as being in agreement or at odds with some other group.

When speaking of American Baptists as Biblically oriented, it would not be helpful to think of them walking in lock-step to a dominant theological drum beat. They are small enough that they can not impose their beliefs on the religious landscape, but large enough to resist compliance to those who can. American Baptists are people of the Word, but they are also a people who engage the Word. This gives them an openness to reading beneath superficial interpretations of scripture.

Another important context is that your author is an Anglo man, who is frankly baffled by the experiences of many people around him. This book does not offer insight to the experience of women in ministry. It does not even suggest strategies for women in dealing with the closed systems of this world. It is born out of a sense of frustration and grief built from the observation that treasured women colleagues are discounted in ministry.

This is not simply an altruistic sentiment. From a strictly selfish perspective, the church, the community, and our personal lives are missing nearly half of the ministry God intends for our blessing. It is a distinct ministry with unique flavor that makes us complete, and we are not complete without it.

Related to this self-interested perspective is a genuine concern for individuals who feel strongly called and have a servant's heart, but find barriers to engaging ministry. Recently a retired male pastor shared with tears in his eyes how incomplete he feels being retired. Aside from issues of self-differentiation, one truth rings clear for him. His very being is connected to doing ministry. He doesn't want to know how to be a whole person apart from ministry. His profound new sense of loss is a painful experience that lurks like a scepter behind many women in ministry. The newness wore off long ago and now it is a dull ache that never goes away.

Some who never receive a call from a church struggle through the emptiness and find other ways to serve. The compassion we hold for the retired pastor should reverberate more deeply in our hearts for the women who simply want to live out God's call on their lives.

One more context of this book is related to its motivation. There is a woman Area Minister who works with churches engaged in pastoral searches. She brought to a church a resource package with the profiles of several excellent potential candidates for their pastoral position. Oblivious to what they communicated to her, they pulled out the profiles of women, pronounced them unacceptable and threw them out unread in front of her.

It must be conceded there are churches simply not prepared to make the step to a new (for them) mental model of ministry. No one wants to send a woman to an impossible place where ministry candidates are disposed of so thoughtlessly. Still there must be something that can be said to a church or a person who is unaware of their own closed mindedness.

When the Area Minister met with her colleagues on her regional team she exclaimed, "Some day a man is going to have to write a book saying it is okay to call a woman into ministry!"

"Why a man?" someone asked.

"Because people simply won't listen to us women. We can sit right there across the table from them and it doesn't mean a thing. If a man says it, it will at least carry some weight," she replied.

This woman Area Minister is a very hopeful person, but this book may not carry as much weight as she would like. Still, on the chance that people want to read the Bible with accuracy and not just the pervasive social bias that marginalizes women, it is offered as a partial fulfillment of her request.

Unfortunately there are a large number of Christians who throw out half the council of God. It is the half to which Acts 2: 17 refers: *Your men servants <u>and</u> your maid servants will prophesy.* In the context of the church today prophecy is what we call preaching. It is the forth telling of God's word. It is the *Thus says the Lord.* Clearly, people who believe the Bible, the whole of Scripture, affirm that women are as called as men by God to preach. It is not either/or; both are to prophesy. Sadly, in the church, the portion of God's Word that advocates ministry for everyone is too often found in the waste baskets full of women's profiles and resumes. This little book is for people who choose to be more faithful with God's Word.

This book is cast like another little stone into our pond of religious ignorance with the hope that maybe someone will use it to gain their footing. If it helps someone receive the blessings God intends him or her to have, then it will have been worth while. If it encourages someone to continue pursuing the ministry God has called her to, it may even be important.

Chapter One
What the Bible Actually Says

Not too long ago I had a conversation that took place with a new church member in one of the larger churches in the Area. Not having been a Christian for very long, John revealed a condition held by many in the church today. He claimed to believe the whole Bible and said it like he meant to defend the claim against all comers.

When asked, "How do you believe it?" he replied, "Just like it is written, cover to cover!"

"Have you read it cover to cover?" was my natural follow up question.

John's zeal was undiminished. "Well not yet," he replied, "but I believe it just the same."

The thought that this kind of commitment to the authority of God's Word ought to be encouraged suggested another follow-up question, "So what do you believe?"

"I believe that we will be raptured and then there will be seven years of tribulation and then the end happens at Armageddon!"

Suddenly encouragement turned to concern. John thought he believed the Bible, but this may not be so. He believed what he heard about the Bible from a class on pre-millenial prophecy. Equally concerning was the level of authority he gave the class and the energy with which he was ready to defend it. Only the Bible is inspired. The class may be inspiring, but it does not have the same authority accorded to the Word of God. Instead of reading the Bible, John reacted to what he had heard others say it meant.

In many parts of American Baptist life this man's understanding of what the Bible says about end times is the most common interpretation, but this book is not about end time studies. This true story serves as an illustration. An honest presentation of Biblical end time study includes the fact that there are other Biblical interpretations of what will be.

John illustrates what happens in the Evangelical community concerning the issue of women in ministry. People believe what they've been told the Bible means, or they've come to an opinion on their own. In either case it is just an opinion and should not be confused with what the Bible actually says. The standard of 'what the Bible actually says' will dominate this book.

When we consider what the Bible says about Women in Ministry, there are at least two voices that have informed our evangelical preconceptions.

These two are:
1. The King James Version of the Bible
2. Past and present cultural understanding of the role of women.

Evangelicals who may have never owned a King James Version (KJV) of the Bible are still profoundly affected by it. Christianity in the United States has been shaped by the lyrical voice of the King James Version. The KJV has become part of our spiritual DNA. There is no doubt that the world is richer for it.

In spite of our love and appreciation for the King James Version, it does have some drawbacks. This is the version that refers to men servants as deacons and women deacons as servants. The authors of the King James Version had several agendas that innocently but profoundly colored what they wrote.

The Bible of course is written primarily in Hebrew and Greek, not Elizabethan English. In Greek, the word deacon means 'servant' or 'minister'. One of the places where the authors of the KJV make the switch is Romans 16:1. This passage serves as the inspiration for the title of this book as well. It says, *I commend to you Phebe our sister which is a servant* (deacon) *of the church which is at Cenchrea.*

The word servant in this passage was written in Greek as 'diakonos'. In I Timothy 3:12 the same word is used in a specifically male context. Now the same word is given special importance and an exact translation is made, *Let the deacons be the husband of one wife, ruling their children and their own houses well.*

So what does the Bible actually say? Many other translators have followed the KJV by subconsciously imposing their social agenda on the Bible. These man-made interpretations give a lower status to women. Still, the Bible clearly and literally places a woman on the same level as men in terms of ecclesiastical title and authority. Romans 16: 2 commands a measure of authority be given to Phebe. The Romans are to cooperate with her, doing what she needs to have done in order to fulfill her ministry. The passage literally reads: ...*that you help her in whatever manner she have need of you; for she herself has also been a good friend to many, and to myself as well.*

Cultural conditioning is the other lens through which we see the role of women in the church. The United States is one of the most progressive countries in the world in terms of equal rights and opportunities for women. This provides some with the false comfort of thinking we are free from gender based cultural bias. Nothing could be farther from the truth.

Several years ago there was a popular riddle that demonstrated the point: *A father took his son who took his son on a fishing trip and on the way they were in an accident. At the hospital the doctor looked at the son of the son and said, "I can't do the surgery, this is my son". Who was the father?*

The answer, of course, is that the father is the father in law of the surgeon. The doctor is the boy's mother. Try the riddle with the people you know. The solution is obvious unless there is a mental block that makes it difficult to think of a woman as a competent surgeon. Scripture prohibiting women as doctors simply do not exist. Here is an example of cultural conditioning against women as doctors. It is an attitude which many use to organize their understanding of the world.

Similarly, many Baptists are not accustomed to thinking about women as pastors. Changing mental models always requires an effort, but some changes are not so difficult as one might fear. Thinking of women as pastors is one such change. People who set their preconceptions aside often experience that some women are excellent preachers and pastors. Far from being painful, it is a very rewarding experience to mentally change our models of gender and ministry, especially if we change them in ways that allow the Bible to come through unfiltered.

Chapter Two
God's blessing

About twenty years ago I was called to a small church of 45 along the Ohio River. It was a beautiful place with precious people overlooking the rich river valley with the hills of West Virginia in the background. The church grew slowly, but steadily for several years. It had nearly doubled in size when Doradean Rinard and her husband Doyle visited.

I had known Doradean for several years. Doradean was in her mid fifties when she came. She was an encourager and on the few occasions when I had seen her at Association and Region meetings. I had come to appreciate her affirming grandmotherly presence. Even more, I appreciated her lively commitment to Jesus. I was excited when she visited our church on the hill.

When I asked how she came to be visiting our church on the hill she began to unfold a story about her call to minister to children. She looked at me as if expecting me to understand her dilemma. I did not. It seemed to me that this would be a great opportunity for any church.

She must have sensed this in me because she explained that when she shared this with her pastor he called a deacons meeting to deal with "the problem". Her pastor and the deacons believed her sense of call to minister to children could not be Biblical, and suspected it was a function of her own ego or perhaps worse, some evil influence intended to split the church. It was suggested that she should leave.

Our little church on the hill was running a comfortable 85 on a Sunday morning, but we wouldn't be able to afford a salary. Nevertheless, Doradean agreed to let me ask if she could be our pastor to children. I was not surprised when they said yes.

There was a surprise however. I did not expect the negative and vocal response that most of the pastors in the area had to our decision. The words 'ministerial malpractice' were used in my presence and I'm sure there were others reserved for my absence. Several churches in the Association heard sermons about women's proper place.

I was young. Older, wiser or at least greyer heads were sure we were wrong. I poured over scripture to see where we were in error. Even when interpreted through the KJV there was nothing that suggested it was inappropriate to call a woman to minister to children. The Bible actually says that everyone is called to minister as are all part of the body of Christ, the church.

Consider for example I Corinthians 12:7:

But to each one is given the manifestation of the Spirit for the common good.

It seemed clear that God had equipped each one of us to make a contribution to the ministry of the church. Why should Doradean, or any other woman for that matter, be an exception?

We licensed Doradean to minister, and the second surprise appeared. The power of God's call was overwhelming. Not knowing what to do with a new staff person, we decided there should be a weekly staff meeting. Pastor Doradean was keenly sensitive to not upset the conservative evangelical heritage she came from, so she brought her husband to the staff meeting as a sort of 'covering'. Her humble submission to a system that had virtually excommunicated her was inspiring. She was about obedient ministry, not about upsetting old mental models or about vindicating her new ones.

At our first staff meeting, Pastor Doradean asked for 75 chairs to be set up for the Wednesday evening program. I wondered at the request. We certainly did not have 75 children in the church and on Wednesday we would be lucky to see half a dozen of the ones we did have.

Reading the misgivings Doradean explained, "I intend to have 75 children at our first Wednesday night this quarter. I'll need 75 chairs for them." Pressed further she also intended to feed them Koolaid and cookies and have them draw and color while she read a Bible story. I thought to myself that I now understood the "problem". These were unrealistic expectations colliding with a lack of planning. Feeding children red dye and sugar and expecting them to draw or color while a story was read appeared to be a recipe for disaster. I just knew I would be fired for leading the church to this point of confusion.

Doradean tried to calm my fears. Her husband Doyle would be there to help and everything would be fine. Besides, she had prayed about it and this is what God was leading her to do. Right then my faithless mind gave me a way out. It occurred to me that there would probably only be six children and what harm would there be in having so many chairs set up? This would be a good learning experience and we agreed to set up chairs on Tuesday evening. I resolved to stand with Doradean through her steep learning curve.

The church sits on a large hill with the sanctuary above the walk-out fellowship hall below. From the sanctuary windows is a commanding view of the hillside full of trees and a few of the houses below. Through the hillside woods is a series of trails that people use to walk up to the church.

Wednesday evening came and while Pastor Doradean was making Koolaid I looked out the windows. A sense of panic swept over me. Streaming up the hill like lines of ants were children, dozens of them. It was clear that 75 chairs would not be enough. I flew down the stairs to help set up more chairs and maybe avert an impending disaster. Doradean was already greeting them. The fellowship hall was packed. Here was a congregation as large as a good Sunday morning. Then the miracle happened. The children sat in the chairs. They had their piece of paper to color. They balanced Koolaid and cookies on one knee and they listened as Doradean told a Bible story.

With a prayer on my lips, I made my way back upstairs to the adult Bible study. It was twice its normal size. Some parents had brought their children and decided to stay. During that long 45 minutes Doradean's Bible story was interrupted every other sentence. A little Koolaid was spilled. Doradean was unflappable. Seven children made a commitment to Jesus Christ. And I was grateful that Doradean stood with me during my own steep learning curve.

That little church had over 150 on Sunday mornings in just a very short time. It might be tempting to say it is because there was a good senior pastor. The truth is, the church grew because the power of God was set free to minister the way He chose. And He chose to minister to children (and the rest of us) through Pastor Doradean.

Chapter Three
Ordination

Some people reflecting on the experience of Doradean Rinard may feel a little like Peter in Acts 10:47. He was forced to admit his theology of the Gentiles was too small for God. Seeing the presence of the Holy Spirit, he conceded, *surely no one can refuse the water for these to be baptized who have received the Holy Spirit just as we did.*

In Doradean's case, as in the case of so many others, the presence and power of God's Holy Spirit is unmistakable. Just like it was for Peter, we might challenge ourselves. Surely no one can refuse to recognize this ministry for those to be ordained who have received the Holy Spirit just as we did.

Ordination in Baptist churches is one of those strange almost extra-Biblical ordinances. There are even some who refuse ordination citing Psalm 111:9 which proclaims, *Holy and Reverend is His name.* Whether or not the Psalms reserve the title for the Lord only, in practice Baptist ordination services are just the church's formal recognition of God's call in the lives of those who are set apart for Him.

In congregational polity God's will is understood in community. It is the gathering of those who carry the Holy Spirit which rules in the church. So ordination is the community's affirmation that the call felt by an individual is genuine.

There are several Biblical precedents for ordination. In a sense the Apostle Paul was ordained when Ananias prayed and laid hands on him in Acts 9: 15-18, though that ordination is not recognized by the believers in Jerusalem until Acts 13:2-3. Here it says:

While they were ministering to the Lord and fasting, the Holy Spirit said, "Set apart for me Barnabas and Saul for the work to which I have called them." Then when they had fasted and prayed and laid their hands on them, they set them free to leave..

The Biblical model for ordination most probably is the laying on of hands. Besides Acts 9: 15 and 13:2 which both refer to Paul, this practice is also noted in Acts 19: 6, Acts 21:27, I Timothy 4:14, Hebrews 6:2 and I Timothy 5:22. The only one of these passages that gives any guidelines for how ordination should be done is I Timothy 5:22 which warns, *Do not be too hasty to lay hands upon anyone.*

The obvious direction of this passage is that ordination should take time. But another message can be drawn out of the verse. What the Bible actually implies is that laying on of hands could be available to anyone only that we not be hasty in doing it. There are absolutely no injunctions about avoiding it for some classes of people. If we believe the Bible means any one when it says anyone, we are forced to support ordination of all, and by this we must mean women as well as men.

Many Christians would agree that women are called to ministry. The disconnect for so many is recognizing that call. Sadly, failure to recognize the call diminishes us. We lose value and benefit because of our failure to affirm what God is doing in our midst. We make that loss official by failing to ordain those whom God has called.

When I became an Area Minister I was called to a part of the American Baptist family that is relatively closed to women in ministry. In this climate was a woman serving as an Associate Pastor. Consistent with my past experience I could see that God was in the business of blessing her ministry.

Most people in the Area appreciated her ministry. She was one of the people who helped run the Area youth committee and the churches shared pride and enthusiasm in the job she did. When she asked about ordination I could not envision any problems.

A pastor not far from the church she served soon helped me understand my naivete. He expressed concern about the unbiblical nature of what we were doing. He did have some scripture which we will discuss in future chapters, but nothing that actually applied to ordination. As he spoke I thought I heard the deacons who had initially asked Doradean to leave whispering in the background.

As the time approached for the ordination council I fretted about having a quorum. When the day came there were several churches notably absent. But there was no need to worry. So many had seen the hand of God in this pastor's life that most churches sent a representative and she was gladly affirmed.

The important part of this story happened after the ordination. This Associate pastor accepted a call to Area ministry and in that capacity helped in the foundation of the Church Planters Institute for National Ministries. There are a growing number of church planters and hundreds of new churches full of thousands of people won to the Lord because her ministry was recognized and empowered. The kingdom of God is vastly larger and richer for the recognition of her ministry.

The church of her detractor is full of wonderful people. No one could say exactly why its attendance fell from 110 to 70 in the year following this woman's ordination. The pastor who was concerned about Biblical purity chaired the Area Youth Committee when she left and it too disintegrated. It was several years after that pastor's departure that the church and the committee recovered.

There is no joy in the failure of a ministry. It would be unfair to say the ministry failed simply because a person opposed recognizing God's ministry in women. What is important to observe is that recognizing God's ministry is linked to receiving God's blessing. It does not matter what is the gender of the container in which that blessing comes.

Chapter Four
I Corinthians 14

It was a beautiful spring Sunday. The trees were just beginning to bud and there was a freshness to the colors along the road. I was scheduled to preach at a church about an hour from my home. There was more than enough time to arrive, even get lost trying to find the church, and still be early in arrival. On the way I rehearsed the sermon, reviewing the points I hoped to make.

The countryside was beautiful; the roads were good and the directions straightforward. Sunday school had not even begun when I arrived. The pastor showed me to a Sunday School classroom. The teacher looked up and said, "I'm so glad you are here! We have saved I Corinthians 14 for today so you could help us." I began to mentally organize my understanding of speaking in tongues as I sat down.

When everyone had assembled and coffee had been passed around, they announced the lesson. What we want to know is "How can we let women speak in church?"

The teacher introduced I Corinthians 14:34 and 35:

Those women are to keep quiet in the churches; for they are not permitted to speak, but are to subject themselves, just as the Law also says. If they desire to learn anything, let them ask their own husbands at home; for it is improper for a woman to speak in church.

Many modern translations actually say "Women keep silent in the churches." This was not part of the peaceful morning I had imagined. What was that scripture trying to teach? Verse 34 and 35 are part of a longer passage beginning in verse 26 and ending in verse 40, and will not be well understood without knowing what the Bible actually says in the larger context. The theme of the passage is in the conclusion of verse 40:

But all things must be done properly and in order.

There were two activities disrupting worship in the Corinthian church. Men were interrupting the service to speak in tongues and women were interrupting to ask questions. In both cases the interrupters are commanded to be quiet. In verse 28 men with a gift of tongues were to be silent unless there is an interpreter and of course there are verses 34 and 35 which command the women to save their questions for later.

The translation 'to be silent' for both of these passages conveys an incomplete meaning from what the Bible actually says in the original Greek. The word that is behind this verse is σιγατωσαν, or in English, *sigatosen*. The root of this word is σιγη, or *sigae*, which means to speak in a hushed tone. *Sigatosen* means to be at peace or to be still. It is quietude, not absolute silence.

In keeping with verses 26, 33 and 40, these services are supposed to be peaceful and without confusion. In this context the silence that men and women are both enjoined to observe means a lack of disruption.

The word for speak in verse 34 and the word for speaking in tongues in verse 26 are also linked. In this instance women speaking are described by the word λαλεω, or *laleo*. Speaking in tongues is γλοσσαλαλεο, or *glossalaleo*. This is speech that in either case could be described as babbling, one coherently, one not. Directed intentional speech like a sermon, prophesy or teaching would be described by the word φθεγγομαι, προφεσεω, or λεγω, which in English would be *ftheggo*, *propheceo* or *lego*.

If the Bible were forbidding women to preach it would have been a different word than the one that is used here. Paul is not addressing issues of who may lead services, but the behavior of the congregation while those services are being led.

So who does lead the services? A few pages earlier Paul gives directions for how services are to be conducted. In I Corinthians 11: 4 and 5 the Bible says:

Every man who has something on his head while praying or prophesying disgraces his head. But every woman who has her head uncovered while praying or prophesying disgraces her head, for she is one and the same as the woman whose head is shaved.

Avoiding for the time being what is on or off our heads, it is clear that both women and men pray and prophesy in church. In a future chapter we will return to issues of whether there is a hierarchy of men over women, but for the time being, be sure that if you believe the Bible you must find a way for women as well as men to pray and prophesy in church.

On the way home from church I reflected on the Sunday School class. Why was it that people would focus on commanding women to silence and miss the verse that commanded men to silence? It was a non-Biblical bias that led them to miss the real point of the Scripture: that everything be done decently and in order. It is time, past time actually, for the church to be moved by a bias that lifts up the ministry God has placed in women. Women are loved and treasured by God. The church should do the same.

Chapter Five
Women in the pulpit

Part of the problem that both men and women have with the issue of women in ministry has to do with their understanding of prophecy or preaching. In our world there are some who draw a line in the sand just behind the pulpit.

Several years ago our Area had the opportunity to invite noted scholar Molly Marshall to be the keynote speaker for our annual meeting. One pastor exclaimed, "If she is going to speak from the pulpit, my church won't be there!"

In actuality it would have been a surprise if that particular church had attended, but the continued conversation was instructive. With some exasperation the pastor asked why we wanted so badly to have women in the pulpit?

"We don't want women in the pulpit!" I exclaimed. Before he was able to speak I continued, "We don't want men in the pulpit either. We want Jesus Christ and Him only, and we'll take Him in any package we can get."

Dr. Marshall blessed hundreds of people during the meeting. She lifted up Jesus Christ and the power of God's Holy Spirit. And yes, she stood behind the pulpit.

Some people have a fear that letting women preach somehow gives them authority. Whatever it is about this they think might be bad, they completely miss the point. The preacher does not dictate. It is a point that will be made again later, but authority resides in the Word, in the Holy Spirit, in the holiness of God, in the lordship of Jesus, in the power of the Blood and never in the preacher.

Many people are seduced by the platform. There is a unique ego boost to being able to tell people how to live their lives every week. It is precisely that ego that must not appear in the pulpit. It is not about being a man or a woman. The preacher's job is to be invisible so that the Word of God can shine through.

It would be nice for people to recognize the tremendous strength that women bring to ministry. However, those who insist women are weaker vessels, should remember that God uses and blesses the weak vessel. For people who marginalize the strength of women, there is little option but to seek out women as preachers. The Bible actually says in II Corinthians, 12: 10 and 4:7

...for when I am weak then I am strong.

But we have this treasure in earthen vessels, so that the surpassing greatness of the power will be of God and not from ourselves;

The point of these passages is that God is seen most clearly when we are weakest. Some actually try to make the case that women are somehow the weaker vessel based on a shallow reading of I Peter 3:7 which says, *You husbands live in the same way (as Sarah obeyed Abraham, verse 6) with your wives according to knowledge, giving honor unto the wife, as to the weaker vessel, and as a fellow heir of the grace of life, so that your prayers will not be hindered.*

There has been too much emphasis on the weakness of women already, but if it is true that women are the weaker vessels, it means that women are the most promising candidates to fill the pulpit. What is also undisputable in this verse is that men who do not honor their wives in whatever area God has empowered the wives, lose the opportunity to be blessed, even to the point of the men not having prayers answered. What is also clear is that on a spiritual level husbands and wives are equal in sharing the grace of life. Being both heirs, it is a matter of sharing, not of one ruling over the other.

Chapter Six
The Fullness of Christ Is Neither
Male Nor Female

Some people say that the church is a foretaste of heaven. To the degree that this is true, the Bible is clear that the distinction between men and women is not helpful. In Matthew 22, Mark 12 and Luke 20 there is the record of a confrontation between the Sadducees and Jesus. In the passage Jesus affirms the resurrection which the Sadducees denied. But like many things in the Bible it actually says something more. Luke 20: 34-36a says:

The sons of this age marry and are given in marriage, but those who are worthy to rise from the dead and attain to that age, neither marry nor are given in marriage; for they cannot even die anymore, because they are like angels...

The same passage in both Matthew and Mark begins with an admonition, Matthew 22:29: *you err, not knowing the Scriptures nor the power of God.*

Focusing on the gender of one who offers ministry in Jesus name misses the One who provides the blessing. Imagine a birthday party at which presents wrapped in the wrong color paper were discarded unopened. The same situation applies to discarding Jesus because He comes wrapped in the 'wrong' gender of person. Is the Holy Spirit less God when he manifests himself in a woman than when he shows up in a man? It would be silly to think that our gender is somehow greater than the power or the nature God.

What the Bible actually says is that these artificial divisions we pay so much attention to do not exist as far as Jesus Christ is concerned. Galatians 3:26-29 not only makes this clear, but adds something to the conversation that needs to be observed:

For you are all sons of God through faith in Christ Jesus. For all of you who were baptized into Christ have clothed yourselves with Christ. There is neither Jew nor Greek, there is neither slave nor free, there is neither male nor female; for you are all one in Christ Jesus. And if you belong to Christ, then you are Abraham's descendants, heirs according to promise.

It is plain that if a person believes the Bible, they no longer have the luxury of categorizing ministry as male or female, but what also appears is the application of the title 'sons of God' to Greeks, slaves and women.

The concept of sonship here and elsewhere is linked to inheritance. When Jesus is referred to as either the son of man or the son of God there is an implicit understanding that He is the one to whom both kingdoms ultimately belong. This is part of the plain meaning of the parable given in Matthew 21:33-46, Mark 12:1-12 and Luke 20:9-19. This is one of only three parables that is recorded in all three synoptic gospels. In it the landowner (God the father) sends his son (Jesus) as the inheritor to collect the rent for a vineyard. The slaves who work the vineyard kill the son in an attempt to seize the inheritance. Beneath the surface of the text is an understanding that Jesus, the Son of God, is destined to inherit all things.

If you remember the story of Jacob and Esau you recall that it is often the first born son that had the right of inheritance. However that did not have to be the case. What is prophetic and unusual about Job in the Old Testament is that according to Job 42: 15 his daughters also inherited. The wonderful promise of John 1:12 is that to *as many as receive Him, to them He gave the power to become the sons of God, even to those who believe on His name*. This sonship applies to women as well as to men.

Those who think that having women in ministry is a problem miss a deeper and more important point. It is a son of God through Jesus Christ who ministers, not a woman or a man. And the title has nothing to do with gender. It is the inheritor who receives what the Father leaves.

When Jesus was crucified and rose from the dead it activated the inheritance laws. Galatians 3 makes it clear that part of that inheritance is faith, but John 14: 12 suggests something more. Here Jesus says:

Truly, truly I say to you, the one who believes in Me, the works that I do, they will do also; and greater works than these shall they do; for I go to the Father.

There is something more than inheriting heaven in the sweet by and by. We inherit the work of ministry in the here and now. The great commission does not belong to some one group, it belongs to every inheritor. Imagine trying to explain to the Father why we took from our sisters something Jesus died to give to all of us.

That which Jesus left behind has an important purpose. Ephesians 4: 12-13 details the reason we have a Spirit empowered ministry. It is:

For the equipping of the saints for the work of service, to build up the body of Christ; until we all attain to the unity of the faith, and of the knowledge of the Son of God, to a mature man, to the measure of the stature of the fullness of Christ.

If we are to attain the fullness of Christ we need to focus on Jesus not gender.

Chapter Seven
A Boy Named Sue

All over the ancient world a woman named June left her name. Sometimes on walls, sometimes scraps of paper, sometimes in books. She was a busy woman, unless, of course, there were very many women named June. We have found hundreds of references to her. In every instance when her name occurs it is a woman to whom reference is being made. We know that partly by the ending on the name but also because some of the extended writings are clearly speaking about women.

No one ever heard of a man named June until after the fifth century AD when a male ending turned up on the end of June's name in a copy of the book of Romans 16:7. Until then the Roman's references also only had female endings. This man named June was as strange as the late Johnny Cash's song *A Boy Named Sue*. Why would someone use an exclusively female name for a man? And why would subsequent translations continue the error?

In all fairness not every subsequent translation used the revised text. One translation that did use it however was the King James Version. The reason why the error was made and then repeated is that the original reading was simply too uncomfortable for people with a prejudice against women in the ministry. Romans 16: 7 reads:

Greet Andronicus and June, my kinsmen and my fellow prisoners, who are outstanding among the apostles, who also were in Christ before me.

Whoever June was, Paul considered her an apostle and not just an ordinary one. She was committed to Christ before Paul's conversion, and was enduring some form of imprisonment for the same reason as Paul. She was a proclaimer of the risen Lord.

What Paul requests of the Romans is substantial. They are called upon to greet June and her compatriots. The Greek word for greet, ασπζομαι, or *aspadzomai*, is very similar in meaning to the English word. It carries a sense of welcome to it. It also carries a sense of recognition. In a formal situation greeting a person involves an introduction and an acceptance of that person. It means inclusion.

That same recognition that Paul requests of the church at Rome is upon us as well. If you believe what the Bible actually says, we must recognize a woman in ministry.

So why have we been burdened with a mistranslation for so long? Whatever problem the person who changed the text had appears not to have been shared by the early church fathers. Many of them knew of June and included references to her in their writings. John Chrysostom writing around 390 AD said in his *Homilies on the Acts of the Apostles and the Epistle to the Romans, XXXI*:

> *But they were of note owing to their works and to their achievements. Oh! How great is the devotion of this woman, that she should be even considered worthy of the appellation of apostle.*

Origen of Alexandria, Jerome, Hatto of Vercelli, Theophylact and Peter Abelard, all early church Fathers understood her to be a woman. It was not until Martin Luther used the one corrupted text from the fifth century which changed her to a man, that anyone took seriously the notion that she was not a woman. Until 1516, the first three fourths of historical Christendom, every popular representation of June acknowledged the fact that she was a woman. If you have to believe a man, believe the people historically closest to her. June the apostle was a woman. Better yet, believe it because the Bible says it.

Actually June is not the only woman to have her gender reassigned. Though not recorded in the Bible there is powerful archeological evidence that the early church also recognized Theodora as a bishop around 450 A.D. Much later church historians made an attempt to record her as being a man. Unfortunately for them there is a mosaic of her which was probably completed while she was still alive in Rome. It clearly identifies her as a woman and you can still visit it in Rome if you are in need of further persuasion.

Chapter Eight
Differences

Roland was a new senior pastor who said he was supportive of women in ministry during the interview. Unfortunately after arriving on the field he had severely restricted the responsibilities of the associate pastor because, "some ministry was not a woman's ministry." This church was situated about forty miles from a small Independent denomination Bible School and Seminary with which the new pastor was associated.

Cheryl was the associate pastor and had been on staff about four years. Not every one in the church had been in favor of calling a woman associate pastor, but Cheryl had done a good job and had earned the appreciation of many of her detractors. However after Roland's arrival it seemed that nothing she did was acceptable. The time had come for her to leave.

As I spoke with Cheryl she seemed to be getting hung up on being a pastor like all the 'guys', so I offered an opinion, "I think there is a difference between men and women in ministry."

I tried to smile my most charming smile, hoping to soften the expected reaction. Our conversations had been open though being asked to leave a ministry created some significant pain that worked its way into our discussion.

Cheryl responded, "What on earth do you mean? I am so tired of people marginalizing women and making them second-class citizens. Roland thinks that I'm only fit to be a youth pastor somewhere or even a children's pastor. Maybe I should only have a women's tea in the afternoon and call it quits!"

Still smiling, hoping to defuse a little of the energy, I replied, "I know, doesn't that sound just like a man?"

"Yes it does! I thought better of you."

I caught my breath and tried once more, "That's exactly my point. It is just like a man. There is a difference between men and women in this whole area."

The pastor had lived so long in a culture that belittled her femininity that she tried to pastor as if she were masculine. Part of her growth as a minister lay in discovering that who she was is a gift, not a burden.

Sadly, Cheryl soon left the church and was replaced by a young man still in seminary. The senior pastor left about a year later.

The tendency to marginalize women is cross cultural and is pronounced in the dominant cultures of the United States. Even women marginalize that which is feminine. When a man becomes assertive in this culture he is leading. When a woman does it she is domineering. When a man extends a listening ear he is seen as compassionate. When a woman does it, people view her as emotional. Men get angry and are accepted. In this culture the same consideration is not extended to women who are described as catty or shrill. Men give advice, women nag. This sort of double standard is not helpful.

The culture we live in may be one of the most affirming in history, though that by no means excuses its many shortcomings. Even in matriarchal societies there is a distinct difference between men and women. When we observe that it is just like a man to marginalize a woman we recognize the fact that men and women are different.

When a woman is called as a pastor she brings a different set of sensitivities to the ministry. She may have the same or even greater capabilities, but the ministry carries a different perspective than a man can provide.

The problem in our culture (and in most others) is not that men's ministry is overvalued. It is that women's ministry is undervalued. Blessing a community of people requires both perspectives.

Not long ago I visited with a young man who said he thought he could not relate to a woman pastor. When asked why, he replied that a woman simply could not understand what a man had to go through. For instance he would not be comfortable discussing things like sexual issues with a woman other than his wife.

Fair enough, but are men pastors any better able to understand what a woman has to go through? The word oblivious comes to mind. How does a man offer insight into the spirituality of childbirth or comfort in situations of barrenness? How is a male pastor uniquely suited to help a woman deal with unbiblical restrictions of her ministry? For a man to identify with a woman's sexuality would even disqualify him from serving in some of the circles which require pastors to be male.

This marginalization of women is something addressed even as early as Genesis 2: 18:

it is not good for man to be alone.

This sentiment is echoed in Ephesians 5: 31:

for this reason a man shall leave his father and mother and shall be joined to his wife, and the two shall become one flesh.

Man without woman is incomplete. Two unique perspectives are required for us to be whole.

Generally these passages and other similar ones are understood in terms of the marriage bond and family. What the Ephesians text adds to that mix is the church.

The dominant meaning of the passage is that the church needs Jesus in order to be complete. Not to be missed is a secondary point. *Because we are members of His body,* (verse 30), there is a sense of unity. Until male and female ministries are wed, there is an incompleteness. Church systems with only male leadership are sterile and able to produce only some of the blessings that Jesus desires.

It is good to keep in mind the modern proverb that every generality is wrong in particular. When people generalize about a woman's ministry or a man's ministry, there will always be significant exceptions. Still there are some things worth observing.

Most of the people in church are women. A major difference between men and women in the United States is that women are far more likely to be interested in spiritual matters than men. There may be a variety of reasons for this difference. It may be deeper spiritual sensitivity, greater need for comfort or to nurture, a stronger drive for community, or perhaps something all together different. Whatever the cause, church is something that women do more intentionally than men. If commitment to church is what we are looking for in ministry, wisdom suggests looking for women to fill ministry roles.

There have been suggestions that women's ministries are more caring, more nurturing, more maternal than men's. Of course, every generalization misses the mark when applied to specific situations, but this generalization also obscures the point. Men care as much, but they do it differently. The physiology of men and women is different.

Women's brains develop more quickly, men mature more slowly. Because of this women tend to think holistically. They are more prone to multitask. Men's brains develop more slowly; they compartmentalize. Men tend to think in categories. They often have a sense of focus. It is not that one is more caring, the care is just expressed in a different way.

The point is, we need both women and men in ministry.

Chapter Nine
Authority

Dorothy's eyes were red, she had been weeping, though she seemed composed when I sat at the table in the fellowship hall with her. There was a cup of coffee steaming in front of her. She looked weary. It was not long before the tears tried to reassert themselves.

Dorothy is devoted to the Lord and has invested her life in teaching the adult Sunday School class in the church. Her call to teach has been life-giving for her and for the church. People look forward to her class. Her new pastor was charming and personable. Unfortunately he thought women should not be allowed to teach men, not even in Sunday School. He had challenged the church with a reading of I Timothy 2:12. His persuasiveness and Dorothy's desire to be obedient to the Lord had convinced her that she should be silent in church. She used to think she was obedient when she was teaching. Deep in her heart she still knew that had to be right.

I got a cup of coffee and joined her. She shared her struggle. It was tearing her heart that she couldn't teach the class. And she was frankly concerned about the welfare of the class as well as her own heart. "I guess I'll have to be silent," she said.

"Is that really what the Bible says?" I asked her. "Show me."

She opened to I Timothy 2:12 and read:

But I do not allow a woman to teach or exercise authority over a man, but to remain quiet.

When she finished I asked her, "So do you believe that Paul personally wanted women to be quiet and that he did not permit women to teach or have authority over a man?"

"Yes of course."

"So do I," I replied, "But do you also believe that Judas betrayed Jesus and hung himself?"

"Yes of course."

"So you have two historical events, one of which you choose to apply to your life and one (I presume) you do not. What is the difference?" I asked.

"Well Pastor says…" began her reply.

Was Dorothy's new pastor side tracked by a voice other than the Lord? I do not mean to marginalize those who honestly feel that Paul's confession was a rule for church life today. It is just that Paul's confession is not necessarily a commandment just because a pastor says so. We are called to be obedient to the Holy Spirit, not some law about what people can and cannot do. And the Holy Spirit was clearly calling Dorothy to teach. Her class knew it, she knew it, everyone did, except it seems for her new pastor.

Dorothy's pastor, Charles, was listening near by. It was clear when he set his cup of coffee down firmly on the table Dorothy and I shared that he was displeased.

"So how do you feel about women pastors?" he challenged.

"I think if you want to keep women from having authority, making them Baptist pastors is a great idea." I replied.

Charles didn't get it. In Baptist churches, pastors have tremendous influence, but no real authority. We have congregational polity which means God's authority is manifested in congregational vote, not in pulpit decrees. We believe an individual is called to submit to the still small voice of the Holy Spirit, not some ecclesiastical decree. That does not prevent the Holy Spirit from using a Biblical sermon to speak to individuals. We just don't want the sermon to take the place of the Holy Spirit.

The sermon is supposed to be a conduit for the Holy Spirit. Unfortunately many pastors think the Holy Spirit's job is to be a conduit for the sermon to get to the congregation. Charles was one of these. He continued to push the concept of pastoral authority in the church. Only a few months later he pushed himself out the door.

Dorothy is teaching Sunday School again. The church has a new pastor. God has been blessing this congregation with a tremendous infusion of growth. It could have been a church lifting up pastoral authority and pushing women ministers down. Instead it is a church that lets all Christians, women too, have ministries and Jesus Christ is lifted up.

Chapter Ten
Who Disciples Whom?

In churches that have congregational government, authority is expressed by God speaking through the congregation. On a personal level however there is a tremendous amount of influence involved in the mentoring and personal discipleship of individuals.

In this section we will examine I Timothy and Titus including the passage in which Paul gives his personal practice regarding discipleship. Before looking at these passages let's take a minute to look at what the Bible actually says about their context.

The Bible contains many stories that include sin, faithlessness and even well meaning but wrong decisions. The classic example used in the last chapter is that Judas hung himself. We don't use that as a normative method of dealing with our unfaithfulness. The Bible also contains some culturally specific passages. Most of us don't draw water from a well and we rarely have an ox stuck in a ditch. The rules governing those situations do not apply in a literal sense to most of modern life.

The passage in I Timothy 2:9 and 12 both begin with a personal reference identifying the following verses as Paul's opinions. In 2:9 Paul says *I want all women to adorn themselves with proper clothing,* and in 2:12 he says *I do not allow a woman to teach or have authority over a man.* These verses are not just culturally specific. If you believe what the Bible says they only represent the opinion of Paul and serve as an historical record of how the early church operated under his leadership.

It may even be that these verses are not meant by Paul to be applied universally. The verb structure in verse 12 makes it possible to read the verse, *I am not allowing a woman to teach...*which would imply that there is a specific situation to which Paul was responding with this restriction. For instance, in a situation where the women of the church were new Christians, it would be inappropriate for them to also be teachers.

In addition it is important to keep in mind some very specific wording in verse 12. This verse is placed in the context of just one woman having authority over just one man. As such, it can not apply to larger gatherings like a worship service or like pastoring a church. This passage and a subsequent passage a few pages later in your Bible can only deal with one on one discipleship.

As a general rule of discipleship however, we should be slow in criticizing these verses. This is especially so in the wake of the public scandal in the Roman Catholic branch of the Christian family and the not so public scandal in many protestant parts of the family. In 2002, a Church Mutual Insurance agent affirmed an average of one incident a week in Kansas of reported sexual ethics violations for the churches they insure.

We do not live with the luxury of innocence. Evil people use authority and influence in the church to prey upon others. Paul is concerned enough about this that he mentions it specifically in II Timothy 3:6,

For among them are those who enter into households and captivate weak women...

There are predators and they aren't lurking 'out there'. They work hard to incorporate themselves into the church so they can gain access to people who are vulnerable.

With this as a background the passages we will look at are I Timothy 2: 12 and Titus 2:3-4. We will look at other verses in I Timothy 2 in a later chapter.

I Timothy 2:12 says: *But I do not allow a woman to teach or exercise authority over a man, but to remain quiet.*

Titus 2: 3-4 says: *Elder women likewise are to be reverent in their behavior, not malicious gossips nor enslaved to much wine, teaching what is good, so that they may teach the young women to love their husbands, to love their children,..*

These passages outline an approach that discourages cross gender discipleship. In Paul's format men do not teach the young women. Women elders do. Women do not teach men. Men do. Even with this kind of caution recent events have made us aware that we must also guard against same sex predators and pedophiles.

Real discipleship at a personal level involves an intimacy we often overlook. II Corinthians 10: 5 says:

We are destroying vain imaginations and every lofty thing that exalts itself against the knowledge of God, and we are taking every thought captive to the obedience of Christ.

Our secret thoughts, fears, needs and drives provide real keys to our hearts. Someone entrusted to hold us accountable in our discipleship is also someone who holds those keys.

The seduction of that intimacy can be overwhelming for both the mentor and the disciple. It is not just the vulnerabilities of the person being mentored that need to be taken into account. The mentor also has a thought life of their own which puts them at risk.

I had lunch with the former pastor of a church in the Area. Rusty had been caught with a wife of a deacon from the church. He confessed to relationships with half a dozen other women in the community.

Rusty poked at his salad, his head bowed. His voice wavered as he spoke about his call to ministry and how much the church had grown while he was pastor. He looked up with tearful pleading eyes, hoping for help to get back into ministry. I was unmoved. But could this person have had a productive ministry if we had a set of safeguards for him? If it were more difficult for people to have access to intimate parts of others hearts, perhaps some damage would be contained.

There is a woman colleague who does an excellent job mentoring male pastors. Her insight and ability to help them grow is a gift. But there are numerous safe guards that she employs to keep the ministry pure. Several pastors in the Area employ what they call 'the Billy Graham rule'. They are never alone with a person of the opposite sex other than their spouse.

Whatever safe guards you employ in ministry, having well established boundaries is not an option. It may not be necessary to use the same ones Paul did, but the issue Paul raises cannot be overlooked.

It also raises one more thought. It is clear that sexuality drives and defines us in powerful ways. Men and women experience that sexuality differently. Those who have authority to instruct must have real familiarity with the dynamics facing the people they mentor.

Since the majority of church members are women, if we really believe the Bible, perhaps we should insist on more women pastors.

Chapter Eleven
Likewise a Woman

One of the most compelling arguments that Women in Ministry must be supported comes from one simple word, *likewise*. The word means that whatever applied to the first person also applies to the second. Another way to think of it is that the second person is just like the first in some regard. *Likewise* appears in many places throughout the Bible. In I Corinthians 7:3-4 and in I Peter 3:7, for instance it is used to give equality to men and women in the marriage relationship.

One place where *likewise* applies to ministry is I Timothy 3:11: *Women likewise must...* One has to ask what they are doing that is like someone else? In this case the 'someone' are men serving as deacons. The passage has to begin in verse 10:

These men must also first be tested; then let them serve as deacons if they are beyond reproach. Women likewise...

In this context special direction is given to women who are likewise serving as deacons *that they be dignified, not malicious gossips, temperate and that they be faithful in all things.*

This list of attributes runs parallel to the one given for men in verse 8. Men deacons are called to have *dignity, sincerity, not being addicted to much wine, or pursuing dishonest gain.* Compared side by side, women deacons and men deacons are to be dignified. They are to use sincere speech and not be malicious gossips. They are to be temperate and not overindulge in alcohol. They must be faithful in all things and should not try to take what should not be theirs.

Whatever else may be said, the Bible clearly calls for women to be just like the men in regard to service as deacons. In service, we should think of women in some ways just as if they were men.

For those who think a woman should not pray aloud in church, it would be good to turn the page of your Bible and consider I Timothy 2:8-9.

Therefore I want the men in every place to pray, lifting up holy hands, without anger and dissension. Likewise I want women to...

The directions for women who are praying have to do with modest apparel rather than wrath and dissension. But the use of the word likewise connects them to the activity in the verse before. Though the directions are gender specific, the activity they engage in is the same. If you believe the Bible, believe that women should pray in every place.

Chapter Twelve
No Respecter of Persons

I met with a colleague at a recent national convention. She is wise, experienced, passionate and capable. She is not particularly tall. Like me, she serves as a resource for churches searching for a pastor.

My friend described a visit to a church search committee, where the chairperson addressed her as "little missy". He was rather tall and in her description of the situation, he loomed over the committee. He was used to getting his way. If a person is spiritually immature it is easy to overlook the things that really matter, especially if those things come packaged in a person with a smaller physical presence.

In the United States the idea that bigger is better is so ingrained in the way we evaluate things, that we use it to evaluate people as well. Noted economist John Kenneth Galbraith who stands six foot two inches, calls this the most profound and least discussed prejudice in America.

When we think of women in ministry this dynamic should not go unnoticed. Women tend to be less tall than men. In this culture it is easy for men to overlook them. Some even believe they don't 'measure up'. On the face of it most people can see how ridiculous it is to judge people by their size. Yet it happens all the time and Christians are as prone to do it as any others.

There are Biblical examples of this dynamic. Israel wanted a king and got Saul who stood head and shoulders above the rest. When Samuel went to Jesse's house to anoint the next king, he started with the oldest. Even Jesse did not consider little David as a possibility until after God had rejected all others.

God sees people differently. What the Bible actually says is in Acts 10: 34:

God is no respecter of persons.

I Samuel 16:7 says:

Man looks on the outward appearance, but God looks on the heart.

John 7:24 says:

Do not judge according to appearance, but judge with righteous judgment.

What would happen to the ways we interpret scripture if women were twice the size of men? We can look at just about any chapter of any book in the Bible to find places where things could change if we had different presuppositions.

For instance, from the first chapter of Galatians we might gather some interesting theology. Galatians 1:10 might be used to define the pleasure of man as against Christianity. If a man likes it, it must be wrong. Galatians 1:15 might be used to incorporate mothers at ordination councils. Perhaps instead of having a sponsor we should have our mother's speak on behalf of the ordinand? Why not limit councils to only people who are mothers? Galatians 1:16 does not describe Jesus as a man, He is a son. What would that emphasis do for the place of Mary in Protestant theology?

These are pointless questions in and of themselves. Women are not on average twice the size of men and we can only guess at the differences that would make. The questions only serve to make us aware that God sees things differently than we do and when we rely on outward appearance we get things wrong.

Issues of outward appearance include several things:

- affluence, James 2:3 says *you pay special attention to the one who is wearing the fine clothes...*

- gender, nationality, and servitude, Galatians 3:28 says *there is neither Jew nor Greek, slave nor free, there is neither male nor female*

- spiritual gifts, I Corinthians 14:4 says *one who speaks in a tongue edifies himself.*

- public prayer, Matthew 6:5 says *do not be like the hypocrites; for they love to stand and pray in the synagogues and on the street corners so that they may be seen by men.*

Of course the list could be longer. In this book the primary concern is the outward appearance of gender. If an opinion about a person's call to ministry is formed based solely on this issue it is in error. We are called to look upon the heart. If we look upon the heart of a Christian hopefully we will see Jesus.

Chapter Thirteen
Who Is to Blame?

Are women the reason for sin? There is a strong undercurrent of belief that they are; though it is rarely expressed. Still it exerts a strong influence over some people's understanding of women in general and women in ministry in particular. Some people believe, though it would be crude to say so aloud, that women are inferior because of the role they played through Eve in the Garden of Eden.

This sort of belief persuades some to believe that women play a second place role in marriage and in the church. These folks misuse five Bible passages to convey a one sided submission in the marriage relationship. These five passages include I Corinthians 11, II Corinthians 11, Ephesians 5, Colossians 3 and I Timothy 2. However, only one of these is offered in the context of ministry. It is I Timothy 2: 13-14:

For Adam was created first, and then Eve. And it was not Adam who was deceived, but the woman being deceived fell into transgression.

What the Bible has to say about this subject is very instructive. Eve was deceived in the garden. In this her sin was different from Adam's which was the sin of disobedience. This is spoken of in one other place as well, though in this context it is not near a passage dealing with ministry. II Corinthians 11:3 is the other example. The fallenness of humanity is at least partly Eve's responsibility and by extension that fallenness is demonstrated in women just as it is in men.

The strange interpretation that humaniy's fallenness is primarily because of Eve and by extension women in general is simply not in the Bible. Two passages of 8 total verses refer to Eve's role in our fallenness. This stacks up against a large number of passages that tell us it is Adam's and by extension men's fault that the human race is in the state it is in.

Romans 5:12-19, I Corinthians 15:21-45, Job 31:33, Isaiah 43:27 and Hosea 6:7 with a total of 34 verses explicitly give responsibility to Adam for the fall. For instance Romans 5: 12-14 says:

Therefore, just as through one man sin entered into the world and death through sin, and so death spread to all men, because all sinned- for until the Law sin was in the world, but sin is not imputed when there is no law. Nevertheless death reigned from Adam until Moses, even over those who had not sinned in the likeness of the offense of Adam...

I Corinthians 15: 21-22 says:

For since by a man come death, by a man also came the resurrection of the dead. For as in Adam all die, so also in Christ all will be made alive.

So who do we believe? Paul in Romans and I Corinthians or Paul in II Corinthians and I Timothy? The fact is, both are correct. When God made the two, Adam and Eve, into one flesh it involved all of creation. It is not just men, it is not just women. Men and women bear the fall together.

So are women unqualified to be ministers because of their participation in the fall? Absolutely! They are every bit as unqualified as all men are. No one is worthy to carry the miraculous ministry of Jesus Christ. All have sinned. Yet by the grace that is given us, God gave each us gifts of ministry, with the intention that every Christian be a minister of that grace, an ambassador of Jesus Christ.

To say that only women are unqualified is simply not an honest reading of the Bible. To think that God's grace is too weak to empower a woman to minister reflects an alarmingly small view of God. To behave as if God's grace applies only to men is narrow-minded thinking at its worst. Even at its best it is not Biblical.

Chapter Fourteen
What Kind of Car Is It?

My daughter, who is usually very level-headed, attends a University several hours away from home. Sarah phoned me with the announcement that she had bought a car. "How," I wondered, "was I going to afford to maintain a car for her convenience at school?" It simply was not in the budget. Stalling for time to think, I asked questions.

"What kind is it?"

"Red!" Sarah enthused.

"Please tell me it's in good condition," I begged.

"I knew if anyone could get it running, you could Daddy!" I'm always in trouble when she calls me Daddy. Sensing that her father was becoming concerned and maybe even alarmed, she continued, "I think she's a girl, but I don't know what her name is yet."

Actually Sarah had made a tremendous purchase, the car cost only $100 and it was in good condition. What was interesting in retrospect is that Sarah thought the car was a girl. I'm more used to thinking of cars as things, things that usually require a lot of money. In other languages, Greek and Hebrew included, most things are assigned a gender. It would not be strange to think of an inanimate object like a car as being female.

The relative lack of a sexually sorted language in English is both a blessing and a curse when we try to understand what the Bible actually says. On the one hand because the English language is not as sexually categorized, we have the opportunity to consider egalitarian roles for women. This may be one of the reasons why English speaking nations marginalize women less than some others do.

On the other hand, because we are not used to sorting things by gender there are times when making sense of the Bible requires an extra effort. For instance, in the last chapter there were five passages that dealt with man as the one responsible for original sin. In actuality there are over 28 references to man sinning or being the source of sin in the gospel of Matthew alone. But these are not males in general, or man as represented in Adam. They are simply a particular man who sinned.

There are other places in scripture when the masculine version of a word is used referring to people in general. Sometimes in English when we speak about man, we mean mankind. Rarely however do we have this problem with other words. In Greek and Hebrew this sort of problem is common.

If the male ending occurs on the word for thief, which in Greek is κλωψ, or *klops*, (from which we get the word *Klept*omaniac), do we mean a thief in general or do we mean that only men can be thieves? Obviously it can not be the latter, stealing is not gender specific.

Sometimes however the ending is important because it signals a male or female gender in literal ways. Klops with a feminine ending would be a woman whose name is 'Thief'.

This may seem a little confusing, but there is an important reason for bringing it up. When drawing conclusions about gender roles, we must examine the possibility that the words the Bible uses have gender specific endings. One place that consideration should occur is I Timothy 3 and Titus 1. The passages are similar and for the sake of brevity we will look at just the passage in I Timothy 3:12:

Deacons must be the husband of one wife, and good managers of their children and their own households.

Some who are unfamiliar with what the Bible actually says argue that since a deacon must have a wife, only men can be deacons. Unfortunately what they miss is that this verse can also be read, *Male deacons must be the husband of one wife...* The female deacons are actually addressed in the preceding verse beginning with the word *likewise*.

Given the undisputable fact that Paul recognized women deacons and apostles, one can only imagine the reaction he would have to our using a passage addressed specifically to men in order to exclude women.

There is a sort of heads I win, tails you lose approach employed by those who are against women. Throughout the Bible they understand man in its generic sense to represent all mankind. But when it suits their purposes they use the word to exclude women.

In the English language it is possible to exercise this sort of argument against men. All of mankind has sinned and fallen short of the glory of God. Therefore we can conclude that only womankind is without sin. Of course this is an unfair argument. Mankind is understood to include women. Only a person with an anti-mankind agenda would seek to make such an argument.

Unfortunately there are people who demonstrate such a bias when they marginalize women. If they were not against women they would be looking for ways to understand the Scripture that affirmed women. It is true that Greek and Hebrew are not always easily translated and understood. However there are plenty of ways to translate and understand the Scripture that lift women up into their place in Jesus Christ. In the long run, understanding Scripture in ways that affirm women in ministry actually carries more textual integrity.

Chapter Fifteen
Politically Correct

In today's world we have begun to become sensitive to the ways language includes and excludes people. This sensitivity was probably not present in the culture of early Christianity. Because Bible writers were not accustomed to thinking in terms of political correctness we should pay special attention to passages where inclusive language is used. This was not something that came easily to people like Paul and Peter. When they used inclusive language they certainly were trying to make a point. It is a point we should not miss.

In I Corinthians 12 Paul writes in verses 4-6:

There are varieties of talents, but the same Spirit; varieties of service, but the same Lord; varieties of effects, but the same God who effects everything in <u>everyone</u>.

Paul is emphasizing the fact that work in the church is done by the Holy Spirit and the Holy Spirit is present in everyone. Actually, in verse 11 Paul explains who determines what person receives which gift. Surprisingly it is not church polity or tradition or even Scripture. The Holy Spirit determines which person receives which gift of ministry. Paul writes:

But these work that one and the same Spirit apportioning gifts of ministry to each individual as he pleases.

The determination about a person's appropriateness for ministry should be made as a consultation with the Holy Spirit on a case by case basis. There are no rules about excluding gender or pigeon-holing one sex to certain ministries and prohibiting other ministries to them.

Paul does not end this lesson in verse 11. In verse 12 he likens every member of the church to a part of the human body. Every one who has received the Holy Spirit is a part of the church and church membership is linked to ministry. Every person has a contribution to make. He makes it clear in I Corinthians 12: 20 and 21 that everyone's ministry is important:

As it is, there are many members and one body. The eye cannot say to the hand, "I have no need of you," nor the head to the feet," I have no need of you." Quite the contrary.

To be a Christian is to be a functioning member of the body of Christ. This means having received the Holy Spirit. Receiving the Holy Spirit means having a ministry and the ministry is determined and empowered by the same Holy Spirit. The only way women can be denied their ministries is to deny that they can receive the Holy Spirit. This clearly is not Paul's intent. He ends the lesson in I Corinthians 12: 28 - 30. Notice the inclusive language:

That is, God has set <u>all</u> within the church to be first of all apostles, second prophets, thirdly teachers, then workers of miracles, then healers, helpers, administrators, and speakers in tongues of various kinds. Are <u>all</u> apostles? Are all prophets? Are <u>all</u> teachers? Are <u>all</u> workers of miracles? Are <u>all</u> endowed with the gifts of healing? Are <u>all</u> able to speak in tongues? Are <u>all</u> able to interpret?

When Paul speaks of *all* as various kinds of ministers we should believe him. That *all* includes women.

A second Bible writer has a different way of including women as integral to ministry. Peter begins the second chapter of his first letter with some striking language. In I Peter 2: 2 he writes:

Like new born children, thirst for the pure spiritual milk of the Word that you may grow up in your salvation.

The word for newborn children is neuter in Greek. All Christians are meant to receive this injunction. What is often missed is that spiritual milk is required to grow in salvation. To put this as delicately as possible, milk does not come from men. The milk-giver's role is necessarily a feminine one.

In verses four and five the lesson for all Christians moves from milk to mortar. Peter writes:

To whom you come, the living Stone, rejected by men but chosen by God and precious to Him; you also like living stones are being built into a spiritual home to be a holy priesthood, offering spiritual sacrifices acceptable to God through Jesus Christ.

Here the symbolism is also inclusive. The home was the one corner of ancient society in which both genders had a nurturing place. Building a house meant that every one was included.

In verses 6 through 8 Peter makes sure we understand that the whole point of milk and mortar is the chief cornerstone, the Lord Jesus Christ. In I Peter 2: 6 the inclusion is continued:

Behold I lay in Zion a chosen and precious cornerstone. The one who trusts in Him will never be ashamed.

Peter clearly means this passage for women as well as men. There is no sorting out, no second class citizens in this family dwelling. Most importantly is the purpose of the milk and mortar. God has made His newborn children into something wonderful. He has made them all into a people with special standing. In verse 9 and 10 Peter writes:

You are a chosen people, a royal priesthood, a holy nation, a people belonging to God, that you should show forth the praises of Him who has called you out of darkness into his wonderful light. Once you were not a people, but now you are the people of God; once you had not received mercy, but now you have received mercy.

Once again Peter uses inclusive language. By referring to Christians as "a people" Peter clearly means to include both men and women. If we are to take Scripture seriously, when a man or a woman trusts in the Lord they actually become part of a royal priesthood. The only way to deny women a place as a priest before God is to deny them a place among the people who have received mercy. Those who deny women a full place in ministry are in a difficult position. If we believe the Bible, we must recognize women as royal priests before God.

Chapter Sixteen
Jesus and Women

For people who are concerned with what the Bible actually says, there is a large body of material from the gospels that relates to how Jesus regarded women. These passages are not directly related to women and ministry. However they do demonstrate a climate of empowerment and liberty for women. These passages serve as a background for ministry.

It would be inappropriate to ignore the fact that when God chose to send His Son into the world to redeem the world, He communicated first with a woman. Mary did not hear about the event second handedly. She wasn't just present when it happened. God trusted her with the good news at its most vulnerable point.

The ultimate proclamation of good news was done by giving birth. It makes one wonder why a woman can not be trusted to handle the good news now.

The Gospel story starts in Luke 2: 36-38 with a prophet named Anna. As an infant Jesus was cradled in her arms as she confirmed the prophecy that Simeon had previously given and which the angels had told to Mary directly. By the time she holds Jesus she is an old woman. She had spent her life in the temple praying and fasting.

In Matthew 5:25-34, Mark 9:20-22, and Luke 8:43-48 Jesus is recorded as healing a woman with an issue of blood. Her particular disease made her unclean; still she thought if she could just touch the hem of His garment she would be well. When she was discovered by Jesus, the prevailing culture required that she be rebuked and perhaps worse.

What happened may have been as great a miracle as becoming well to her. Jesus said in Matthew 5:22, *Daughter, take courage, your faith has made you well.* Instead of a rebuke she received encouragement and served as an instructive demonstration of faith.

It was a much different situation with the woman taken in adultery. John 7: 53 - 8: 11 relates the tale. In this context the accusers could have brought the man involved in adultery, but like today, the religious system was skewed by cultural prejudice. Not so with Jesus. When asked what to do with the woman, he wrote something in the sand, eventually telling the crowd in John 8: 7, *he who is without sin among you, let him be the first to throw a stone at her.* To the woman He said in verse 11, *I do not condemn you either. Go and sin no more.*

Women may be as culpable as men, but they are not more so. In this passage God's grace certainly was sufficient to redeem the woman. It was a similar situation with the woman at the well. She was not well thought of because of her having had so many husbands. Yet upon meeting Jesus she evangelized her town, proclaiming that she had met the Messiah. You will find an account of her story in John 4: 1-30

Curiously, all the people in the gospels who ministered to Jesus were women. There are two separate episodes both involving an anointing of Jesus feet.

The first woman was Mary, the sister of Lazarus. There are three accounts of the ministry she had, preparing Jesus for His burial. They occur in John 12:1-9, Matthew 26: 6-13 and Mark 14: 3-9.

In Mary's case the ministry of a woman was controversial. The objection lifted up against this woman in ministry was financial, it cost too much money. No one questioned the appropriateness of a woman doing ministry, so long as it did not cost too much. Jesus words should be heard by critics today. John 12: 7 records them, *Let her alone…*

There is another account of a woman ministering to Jesus in Luke 7: 36-50. This was a ministry of greeting for a weary traveler, but the woman turned it into much more. She worshipped Jesus.

Again the objection was not that she should minister to Jesus, or that she seemed to worship him. She had a poor reputation and the objection was that it was inappropriate for Jesus to let her, in particular, near Him. Jesus not only defended her, he used her ministry to teach the others about faithfulness and forgiveness. He sent her away with her sins forgiven.

These are not the only times when women were used as an example of righteous giving and faith. Matthew 15: 21-28, Luke 21:4-5 and Mark 7: 24-30 speak of a Canaanite woman begging for her daughter's deliverance from demons. Initially Jesus turned her away, but her humble persistence was credited by Jesus as an illustration of faith and the reason He answered the prayer.

Mark 12:41-44 and Luke 21:4-5 both relate an incident in which Jesus used the giving of a woman to teach about sacrificial giving. The widow's mite was more than the contributions of the rest of the givers because it was given from want and not abundance. Curiously every example of men's giving are examples from the negative. We ought not be like the rich young ruler. It is better to be like the woman.

There are many other passages illustrating the positive role in which Jesus cast women. One which we have already mentioned is often overlooked by Protestants and should be included. Mary gave birth to the Savior. Some think that women will be saved by childbirth. The fact is, no one is saved without it.

Without recounting the whole miraculous story of the birth of God within humanity, it was a woman who played that pivotal role. Trusted with this much, should not women be trusted with the smaller things of ministry in churches?

Chapter Seventeen
The Women Disciples

One of the churches in the Area has a program based on AWANA. It is slightly different and the curriculum was developed by the pastor. I attended one Wednesday and was pleased to listen to memory verses which the students are assigned to learn. One child who was about seven years old rattled off the names of the twelve disciples from Matthew 10:2-4. "What about the other disciples?" I asked when he had finished.

"What other disciples?" he eyed me suspiciously.

"Well the women disciples of course."

"Silly!" he exclaimed. "There weren't any women disciples."

Actually there were. They are not listed as members of the twelve, but scripture gives far more time to some of them than it does some of the twelve. The list of the women disciples is given in Luke 8:1-3. Here it says,

The twelve were with Him <u>and</u> also some of the women who had been healed of evil spirits and sicknesses: Mary who was called Magdalene, from whom seven demons had gone out, and Joanna the wife of Chuza, Herod's steward, and Susanna, and many others who were contributing to their support out of private means.

We can not speak of the twelve without the '*and*' that appears immediately afterward. Mary Magdalene, Joanna and Susanna were the ones who financed the ministry. They were not the only women who accompanied Jesus throughout the ministry. There is also Mary the mother of James, Mary and Martha and of course Mary the mother of Jesus. It is unlikely that any of these women remained with Jesus throughout the whole ministry. This may be one of the reasons that they are not included in the twelve.

Still these seven occupy an important role. When the men were betraying, denying and hiding in an upper room, a portion of these women were attending the cross and the tomb. Who is it that heard the last words Jesus uttered? Some of those words were addressed specifically to the women. Luke 23: 27- 28 records them:

Following Him was a large crowd of people, and of women who were mourning and lamenting Him. But Jesus turning to them said, "Daughters of Jerusalem, stop weeping for Me, but weep for yourselves and for your children…

A number of these same women arrived at the tomb on the day of Resurrection. Luke 24: 10 gives their names:

Now they were Mary Magdalene and Joanna and Mary the mother of James; also the other women with them were telling these things to the apostles.

Immediately afterwards Mary Magdalene became the first witness of the Resurrection and the first evangelist. Her mission field? She is the one who evangelized what was left of the twelve. Without the preaching of this woman, none of the men would ever have had the chance to proclaim Christ's arising.

So why are these people overlooked as key players in the Gospels? Mary Magdalene shows up more often in the Gospels than all but four of the twelve, more often in fact than Matthew, James son of Alpheus and Thaddeus combined. Peter is the only person to play a larger role in the Gospels than does Mary the mother of Jesus. Mary the mother of James is spoken of more often than Simon the zealot and Bartholomew combined. Mary the sister of Lazarus appears exactly as often as Thomas, though she is not quite the doubter that he was, and these are just the 'Marys' of the group.

If we are looking for what the Bible actually says about women in ministry, we must conclude that the Gospel record is as much about the ministry of women as it is of men. It is not that scripture should be weighed by the number of verses given to each gender. What is striking is that every instance of a woman in ministry is positive. There are no doubters, denyers, betrayers, fearful people or men of little faith in this lot. Weigh scripture if you want, but know this: women in ministry is the field of spiritual quality throughout the Gospels.

Chapter Eighteen
Women in Acts

It is not only in the gospels that women play an important role in ministry. Some people credit Peter with being the founder of the church in Acts chapter 2. To do that they must read past Acts 1:14:

These all with one mind were continually devoting themselves to prayer, along with the women, and Mary the mother of Jesus, and with His brothers.

If this was not 'the' unifying presence for the pre-Pentecostal church, it certainly was a unifying presence. Mary the mother of Jesus is a focal point whom the remnant of the twelve joined in one mind to devote themselves in prayer. Though not named individually, a noted feature in this gathering are *the women*. The pronoun indicates that it is not just any women, or women in general; this is a specific group. It is not unreasonable to think it is the seven women disciples, though this is by no means certain. What is certain is that the book of Acts does not exist without an affirmation of women in a core ministry position from the beginning of the church.

One early example of women in ministry occurs in Acts 9:36. Dorcas who has been a disciple for a while, lives out her life doing acts of mercy. While this is not a pulpit sort of ministry, her testimony made a difference in her community and beyond. When she dies Peter raises her back to life in the first resurrection after our Lord's. In this she serves in a position similar to Lazarus. The last one raised before the Resurrection was a man. The first one raised after was a woman.

Lydia the merchant shows up in Philippi. When Paul goes there Acts 16: 13 records that he began the church planting effort by finding the women outside the gate and talking to them. Lydia opens her heart and she along with her house are saved and become sponsors of the church to whom the letter of Philippians is later addressed.

In Ephesus, Priscilla and her husband are the ones who taught Apollos who was from Egypt. Not restrained from teaching or having authority over a man, the gospel ministry was amplified because of this woman's ministry. Apollos was able to powerfully refute the Jews and demonstrate by the Scriptures that Jesus was the Christ when he went to Achaia because of Priscilla and her husband.

Priscilla's influence is profound. She is spoken of in Romans 16:3; I Corinthians 16:19; and II Timothy 4:19.

Far from prohibiting her from doing ministry, Paul was interested in promoting her ministry in Jesus Christ.

Actual proclamation of the word was attributed to the four daughters of Philip the evangelist. In Acts 21: 8 it says, *Now this man had four virgin daughters who were prophets.* As with all the other women in ministry in Acts, their calling was recorded without reservation as though it was the most natural thing in the world for them to be about the work of ministry.

Clearly Acts revolves around the ministry of Paul more than any other. However no one is suggesting that only Paul be allowed to minister. Around the pivotal point of the beginning church the contribution of women in leadership was welcomed. It should be welcomed now as well.

Chapter Nineteen
Women Leaders in the Old Testament

When discussing women in ministry in the Old Testament, it is tempting to just observe Psalm 68:11 and move on. The Psalm says:

The Lord gives the command; The women who proclaim the good tidings are a great host:

Two things should be beyond argument for those who have an inclination to take the Bible literally. First, there are a lot of women called to preach. Second, this is the Lord's command. Opposing women preaching places us in direct disobedience to God.

There are far too many women leaders in the Old Testament to list them all in this little book. Some of them were Godly and some of them, like their male counterparts, were not. The concept we want to lift up in this chapter is that the idea of women in ministry is not just a New Testament phenomenon. It has deep roots in a long history of women empowered by God to bless the people called by His name.

The temptation is to list a long line of leaders from Eve to Esther and show how they ministered, from the mother of all living to the intercessor before the king depicting the ministry of Jesus. However, people who care about what the Bible actually says are probably already familiar with women like Deborah the judge, Miriam the prophet and even the Queen of Sheba. The point of this book is that many have overlooked the fullness of what the Bible says and simply skimmed over most of the parts pertaining to women. So instead of a long list, consider just a few persons as a starting point.

Lee Anna Star, in her book, *The Bible Status of Women* reports that Rabbinical literature tells of a woman who taught in the School of Prophets in Jerusalem during the reign of King Josiah. Her name was Hulda.

The Bible does not actually reference a School of Prophets in Jerusalem. But curiously in II Kings 22:14-20 and II Chronicles 34:20-32 it does mention a woman named Hulda living on the outskirts of Jerusalem in what was called the 'second quarter'. She was married to Shallum, the 'keeper of the wardrobe'.

When King Josiah was 26 years old he began to refurbish the temple. During the process the book of the law was discovered. As it was read to him, King Josiah began to grieve. It was clear the nation had been living in defiance of God and that could only be bad for any nation. In II Kings 22: 13 the king said to Hilkiah the priest:

Go inquire of the Lord for me and the people and all Judah concerning the words of this book that has been found for great is the wrath of the Lord that burns against us, because our fathers have not listened to the words of this book to do according to all that is written concerning us.

Both Jeremiah and Zephaniah were nearby. It is possible that if there really was a School of prophets Jeremiah at least may have participated. So who did Hilkiah seek out to find the Word of the Lord? Verse 14 continues:

So Hilkiah the priest, Ahikam, Achbor, Shaphan, and Asaiah went to Hulda the prophetess...

When God wanted the nation to hear, He used a woman. Men were available to give the message, but Hulda the prophet was the one He chose.

The next person is unnamed. You will find her story in II Samuel 20:16-22. This historical incident serves as a reminder that to rebel against the king is sin and brings condemnation. In this case the rebel was named Sheba, son of Bichri. Condemnation was brought by Joab the captain of David's army. He encamped against the city of Abel Beth-maacah where there lived a person the Bible calls a wise woman and where Sheba had taken refuge. The offering she gives to appease the judgement is a bit gruesome by modern standards, nevertheless she provides a picture of the final judgement and of deliverance for her people.

It is no mistake that the book of Proverbs depicts wisdom as a woman. Proverbs 4: 5-6 says:

Acquire wisdom! Acquire understanding! Do not forget nor turn away from the words of my mouth. Do not forsake her and she will guard you; Love her, and she will watch over you.

The wise woman of Abel Beth-maacah demonstrates a wisdom ministry without which the city would have been destroyed. The words bear repeating for other ministries of women. Do not forsake her and she will guard you too.

Chapter Twenty
Traditional Women's Roles

We are accustomed to believing that the world of the Bible is largely a man's world. In this world men tend to business and women tend to children. Since the Bible gives an unvarnished look at the history of the past and since there are times when male dominance has been the rule, it would be surprising if we did not see some of that in the Bible.

There is something else to see as well. Though this does not apply specifically to women in ministry, there is a strong affirmation of women in business roles that are beyond traditional patrician models.

We have already mentioned Lydia who was a cloth merchant in Thyatira with a branch office in Philippi. Priscilla along with her husband was a tentmaker. Perhaps the greatest affirmation occurs in Proverbs 31: 10-31. A virtuous woman breaks free from the social typecasting and runs an agribusiness and is a merchant. She manages servants, she is strong, industrious, a real-estate broker who looks forward to the future.

The husband of a virtuous woman derives his standing from her strength. This is much different from the situations where a woman is introduced as the wife of her husband. Here the man is known as the husband of the virtuous woman.

There are many roles for men and women. The problem is type casting people and not allowing them liberty to be what God has called them to be. Must women only tend to children and men only to business? Not if you believe the Bible. Ministry within a family is a high calling to which both men and women should respond. However, God is calling women as He does with men to do something outside of the family. How foolish it would be to stand in the way.

For many Baptists the concept of Women in Ministry is actually the traditional idea. It was not until Scofield published his version of the Bible in 1909 that the concept fell into disfavor. One of his motivations may have been groups like the Salvation Army who published a book by Catherine Booth entitled *Female Ministry: Woman's Right to Preach the Gospel,* in 1859. People like Dwight L. Moody took for granted that women should be in the pulpit. Imagine what he must think about the Institute that bears his name recently repudiating women in ministry.

According to Susan Hyatt's book, *In the Spirit We're Equal*, it was the revivals of the 1800's that gave impetus to the women's suffrage movement. People have forgotten that Christian tradition in America actually affirmed women. Until Scofield, having women in ministry may have been the exception, but it was a happy one. Even fundamentalists like the American Conference of Undenominational Churches, the fore runner to the denomination called Independent Fundamental Churches of America, IFCA, accepted ordained women as pastors. In 1930, 13 of the 174 ordained members were women who carried the title Reverend.

One of the churches in the Area I serve had a woman pastor in the late 1800's. It was the church's best years. The church was packed, the community was blessed and Jesus Christ was lifted up. The years since have been hard on the church. In the last several years the church suffered a split and now attendance hovers around forty.

When they were looking for a pastor they received names of several women who were willing to come for the amount they could afford and who would give them terrific ministry. One would think this church, remembering the tradition of vitality that women in ministry have given, would be open to calling another woman.

"We just aren't used to this new idea of having a woman pastor," they said as they took a vote to consider whether to look at all the profiles before them. A third of the people dissented and fearful of anything that looked like another split, they backed away.

Even churches that should remember do not. Women in ministry is not a new idea. God has always called women into ministry. The new idea, a bad one at that, is not listening to God. In this case they did not even give God a chance to speak.

Recently another church faced the issue. A woman in the congregation was preparing to be licensed for ministry. The congregation had a woman as a pastor during World War II. But there were several in the church who resisted the idea of licensing a young woman to begin ministry. Happily the church voted to affirm her and in the year following she has led nearly a dozen youth and children to the Lord. At the end of her very first sermon three people responded to the altar call and surrendered their lives to Christ. For people who rejoice in building the Kingdom, affirming this ministry makes perfect sense.

Chapter Twenty-One
Contemporary Women

Loren Cunningham relates a story in his book, *Why Not Women,* about visiting his friend Corrie ten Boom on her eightieth birthday. 'Aunt' Corrie invited him to come pray for her because she felt God was leading her to start a new ministry. This woman has preached, written and witnessed to millions. How much richer is the kingdom of God because of her ministry.

Like the observation about the Old Testament, there are simply too many women to try to include in this book. Perhaps just a few stories will help get the point across. God is in the business of using women to do His work.

For example, Watchman Nee was led to the Lord by a woman evangelist, Dora Yu. Watchman Nee produced some of the best known devotional classics of this age. It happened because of a woman in ministry.

One of the exceptional women of faith is Joni Erickson Tada. You may have heard her on the radio. Her testimony of the life of Christ poured through her in spite of being a paraplegic has inspired people the whole world over. Can anyone really say that the people won to the Lord through her ministry are not the most important sign that she is called of God? Would we rather not have had those people won to the Lord?

Joni boldly professes that there are many things that make her unable. But Jesus Christ makes her able. He is greater than the constraints of the flesh. On top of the burdens she cheerfully bears, the last thing she needs is the burden of someone telling her that her ministry is somehow inappropriate.

Recently Anne Graham Lotz spoke at a meeting of the American Baptist Evangelicals during the Biennial convention in Richmond, Virginia. This is the person that Franklin and Billy Graham both say is the best preacher in the family. She lifted Jesus Christ and called us to dependence on the Holy Spirit. People left feeling they had heard from God. It is not that Anne Graham Lotz is God, but she is called and empowered by Him. It is the kind of ministry of which we need more, not less.

These four brief illustrations of faithful women ministers are described by those who marginalize women as just an exception to the rule that ministers should be men. Still, even if you believe that, they are such positive exceptions that we ought to make room for more. The fact is, the reason there are not more is not because God has not called more. It is because people with an agenda to hold women back have misinterpreted Scripture and closed their ears to the still small voice who affirms ministry in all Christians.

When speaking of contemporary women in ministry it would be a mistake to look only to famous people. Because women are overlooked many who should be well known simply are not. A better place to look for the example of contemporary women in ministry is in your immediate life. God has surrounded each of us with women of faith, who love the Lord and know the Word. We are all surrounded by powerful but quiet ministries that take place not up front, but often behind the scenes. If we are in the business of lifting up Jesus Christ, it is time to remove the veil that hides these gifts of ministry and the ministers who bring them. There are women around each of us called and equipped for ministry. Some have already begun to find ways to serve. Affirm them.

Bibliography

Bilezikian, Gilbert, *Beyond Sex Roles: What the Bible Says About a Woman's Place in Church and Family,* Baker Book House, 1993.

Boomsma, Clarence, *Male and Female, One in Christ,* Baker Book House,1993.

Booth, Catherine, *Female Ministry: Women's Right to Preach the Gospel,* Salvation Army Supplies Printing and Publishing Department, reprinted 1975.

Bristow, John, *What Paul Really Said About Women: An Apostle's Liberating Views on Equality in Marriage, Leadership, and Love,* Harper and Row, 1988.

Cunningham, Loren, Hamilton, David, *Why Not Women?,* YWAM Publishing, 2000.

Dickie, Lois, *No Respecter of Persons,* Exposition Press, 1985.

Grenz, Stanley, Kjesbo, Denise, *Women in the Church,* Intervarsity Press, 1995.

Groothuis, Rebecca, *Women Caught in the Conflict: The Culture War between Traditionalism and Feminism,* Baker Books,

Gundry, Patricia, *Woman Be Free! Free to be God's Woman,* Zondervan 1977.

Gundry, S., Beck, J., Blomberg, C., eds *Two Views on Women in Ministry,* Zondervan, 2001.

Hull, Gretchen, *Equal to Serve: Women and Men Working Together Revealing the Gospel,* Fleming H. Revell Company, 1991.

Hyatt, Susan, *In The Spirit We're Equals,* Hyatt International Ministries, P. O. Box 764463, Dallas, Texas, 75376, 1998.

Kroeger, Richard, Kroeger, Catherine, *I Suffer Not A Woman,* Baker Books 1998.

Lutz, Lorry, *Women as Risk Takers for God,* Baker Book House, 1999.

Massey, Lesly, *Women and the New Testament,* McFarland and Company, 1989.

Mohney, Nell, *From Eve to Esther,* Dimensions for Living, 2001.

Star, Lee Anna, *The Bible Status of Women,* New York Lithographing Corporation, 1955.

Trull, Audra and Joe, eds., *Putting Women in Their Place*, Smith and Helwys Publishing, 2003.

Tucker, Ruth, *Women in the Maze: Questions and Answers on Biblical Equality,* Intervarsity Press, 1992.

Zinserling, Verena, *Women in Greece and Rome,* Abner Schram, 1973.

Appendix
Index of Cited Scripture

About the Author

Arthur Jaggard is an ordained American Baptist Minister in Southeast Kansas where he works on the denominational staff. He is a Fellow in the Oxford Society of Scholars and recently completed a Merrill Fellowship at Harvard. He says he likes bright colors and old cars, but his greatest passion is for his wife and children. He is unashamedly devoted to Jesus Christ and is strongly committed to living what the Bible actually says.

Printed in the United States
27420LVS00002B/268-336